Keep Yourself Safe
on the Internet

Don't Be a
Cyberbully

Anthony Ardely

PowerKiDS press.

NEW YORK

Published in 2018 by The Rosen Publishing Group, Inc.
29 East 21st Street, New York, NY 10010

Editor: Greg Roza
Book Design: Rachel Rising
Interior Layout: Michael Flynn

Photo Credits: Cover, p. 5 Hero Images/Getty Images; cover, pp. 3–4, 6, 8, 10, 12, 14, 16, 18, 20, 22–24 (background) Creative Mood/Shutterstock.com; p.7 2xSamara.com/Getty Images; p. 9 Lopolo/Shutterstock.com; p. 11 wavebreakmedia/Shutterstock.com; p. 13 Monkey Business Images/Getty Images; p. 15 Rebecca Nelson/Moment/Getty Images; p. 17 ClarkandCompany/E+/Getty Images; p. 19 KK Tan/Shutterstock.com; p. 21 Timothy OLeary/Shutterstock.com; p. 22 (laptop computer) Digital Genetics/Shutterstock.com; p. 22 (cyberbullying illustration) Trueffelpix/Shutterstock.com.

Cataloging-in-Publication Data

Names: Ardely, Anthony.
Title: Don't be a cyberbully / Anthony Ardely.
Description: New York : PowerKids Press, 2018. | Series: Keep yourself safe on the internet | Includes index.
Identifiers: ISBN 9781538325759 (pbk.) | ISBN 9781538325032 (library bound) | ISBN 9781538325766 (6 pack)
Subjects: LCSH: Cyberbullying--Juvenile literature. | Internet--Moral and ethical aspects--Juvenile literature.
Classification: LCC HV6773.15.C92 A73 2018 | DDC 302.34'302854678--dc23

Manufactured in China

CPSIA Compliance Information: Batch #BW18PK For further information contact Rosen Publishing, New York, New York at 1-800-237-9932.

Contents

Don't Be a Bully

You can do lots of things online. You can do homework and **communicate** with friends. Just like when you talk to people in person, it's important to be nice online.

Being nice means you **consider** other people's feelings. Other people should consider your feelings, too.

It's wrong to hurt other people's feelings. A bully is someone who hurts other people's feelings on purpose. It's never nice to be a bully.

9

You may find bullies at school. You may find bullies online, too. Online bullies are called cyberbullies.

Think Before You Type

Someone may be mean to you online. Don't say something mean back. That would make you a cyberbully, too.

If someone cyberbullies you, tell them to stop. Tell an adult if you're being cyberbullied. The adult will help you. They can help you make the cyberbully leave you alone.

15

Take a minute to think before you say anything online. Calm down if you're angry. This will stop you from saying mean things and becoming a cyberbully. You should never be mean.

Stop Cyberbullies

If someone tells you a secret or **private** fact, don't share that secret online. That would be cyberbullying.

19

Everyone makes mistakes. Say you're sorry if you hurt someone's feelings online, even if it was an **accident**.

No one should make others feel bad online. Be nice and don't be a cyberbully. That will help you and others stay safe on the Internet!

Glossary

accident: Something that is not planned and is not done on purpose.

communicate: To share thoughts and feelings with other people.

consider: To think about carefully.

private: Not meant for other people to know.

Index

Websites

Due to the changing nature of Internet links, PowerKids Press has developed an online list of websites related to the subject of this book. This site is updated regularly. Please use this link to access the list: www.powerkidslinks.com/kysi/cybe